Jacob Kainen

Prints, A Retrospective

Published for the National Collection of Fine Arts

by the Smithsonian Institution Press, City of Washington, 1976

Exhibition November 19, 1976-January 16, 1977
National Collection of Fine Arts, Smithsonian Institution
and
May 24-June 26, 1977
The Baltimore Museum of Art

Library of Congress Cataloging in Publication Data

Kainen, Jacob.
   Jacob Kainen: prints, a retrospective.

   Catalog of an exhibition at the National
Collection of Fine Arts, Smithsonian Institution,
Nov. 19, 1976-Jan. 16, 1977, with text by
Janet A. Flint.
   Includes index.
   1. Kainen, Jacob. I. Flint, Janet A.
II. Smithsonian Institution. National Collection of
Fine Arts.
NE539.K25F55   769'.92'4   76-608286

For sale by the Superintendent of Documents
United States Government Printing Office
Washington, D.C. 20402
Price: $4.00   Stock number: 047-003-00045-8

Photographic Credits

References are to checklist (CL) numbers. Photographs are courtesy of:
The Baltimore Museum of Art, WPA prints, CL nos. 4, 21
Collection of The Newark Museum; Armen Photographers, CL no. 28
The Metropolitan Museum of Art; Gift of WPA, 1943, CL no. 30
Prints Division, The New York Public Library; Astor, Lenox and Tilden
Foundations, CL nos. 9, 14

Cover: *Self Portrait with Drypoint Needle,* 1945, drypoint, cat. no. 14.
Frontispiece: *Hesperus,* 1974, color lithograph, cat. no. 52.

Contents

Foreword

Jacob Kainen is one of those rare individuals who knows a great deal about a great many things and is master of many skills, yet reveals his knowledge only when prodded with a pertinent question. This is not a matter of timidity or excessive modesty on his part, but of an eagerness to know and experience always more rather than to feed on past accomplishments. His prints and paintings have much the same character. They do not bristle with modish style or personal formula, or hint at occult meanings or studious inferences, but continuously open up cannily proposed hypotheses for new awarenesses and enjoyment.

At a rather early point in his career, Kainen became the promoter of others' talents. As curator at the Smithsonian he built up an astonishing collection of prints by past and present artists that was evidence of an extraordinary subtlety and catholicity of taste. But the more he came to recognize and appreciate the quality of others, the more he came to know himself. He never ceased to be an artist, an artist living not in competition but in fellowship with artists of history and of his own day. His is an optimistic art, not because it points the way to social reform but because it expresses and encourages a faith in art.

I know that the term "life enhancement" is old fashioned—it was popularized by Bernard Berenson in those persuasive little books he published in the 1890s—but the phrase seems apt. To be life enhancing, however, art is not bred from art school formulas or artistic stock-in-trade. It is based on a profound knowledge of and respect for life itself. Not an escape, it is a hymn to survival, to the perpetuation of human sensibility.

Jacob Kainen's recent works seem so easy and inevitable that they almost go unquestioned, yet they have impressive staying quality. Like the man himself they embody a rich fund of experience and reveal the depth of their supporting knowledge only through more than casual acquaintance. They invite one, moreover, to share a confidence in exploration and hence a delight in the unexpected and the new.

It is a special privilege to be able to pay tribute to a man who has spent so much of his life paying tribute to the talents of others, and to recognize that his own works stand in easy fellowship with the best of them.

Joshua C. Taylor
Director,
National Collection of Fine Arts

Figure 1.   Jacob Kainen working at Landfall Press in Chicago, 1975.

Jacob Kainen: Prints, A Retrospective

Janet A. Flint
Curator,
Department of Prints and Drawings

One critic has said that Jacob Kainen is "one of the very few American painters of the last decade and a half who have understood precisely what experiment is and how it is used." [1] The development of Kainen's art over more than four decades has indeed been one of experiment and discovery, charted by a self-reliant, imaginative invention and distinguished by a willingness to give up the security of a mastered convention for the sake of new expression. You have the sense that each new painting or print has been approached with the idea that it will be better—closer somehow to the original vision than the one that came before it. To avoid the easy, to permit one's self-conscious free play, to "take the plunge into enigma" involves risks. But Jacob Kainen has always been willing to take those chances. As he said more than twenty years ago,

> I want nothing upon paper or canvas but the open confession of my struggle to express that which has no preexistence but which inheres in my total organism. The results are admittedly unpredictable, but whether I succeed or not is unimportant; the spirit that animates the work is all that finally counts. If this is fresh and eloquent, the work will delight and ring true, and all imperfections will take on the pathos of ruins. [2]

Consequently, each phase of Kainen's work has not always been part of a steady, coherent development; he has chosen rather to follow the much harder path of a self-questioning search that has meant shifts, changes, and reexaminations of personal expression. What has remained constant is his total commitment.

Jacob Kainen was born in Waterbury, Connecticut, on December 7, 1909, one of three sons of a Russian immigrant couple. Around 1919 the family moved to New York City where Kainen's father, an inventive and gifted mechanic, continued his work as a toolmaker. The move opened up new opportunities for Kainen to pursue an early interest in art and by the age of sixteen he was studying with Kimon Nicolaides at the Art Students League. Between 1926 and 1929 he studied at the New York Evening School of Industrial Art, and in 1930, at age twenty, graduated from Pratt Institute in Brooklyn. Perhaps more important for his development during these early years, however, were his explorations of the New York museums and galleries. At the Metropolitan Musum of Art and the Lenox Collection of the New York Public Library, Kainen copied the paintings of Claude, Rembrandt, Constable, and others, and in the galleries absorbed much from studies of both old and recent works. These self-taught lessons in seeing and sensing helped to sharpen his insights and strengthen a confidence in his own opinions. Even from this early period, Kainen was to rely more on independently achieved perceptions than on the didactic lessons of formal instruction.

9

Kainen's graduation from Pratt was followed by several years of painting on his own while he supported himself with occasional odd jobs as counterman in a waterfront café, sign painter, or medical draftsman. The economic hard times of the depression were years of crisis for almost everyone. For the young artist searching for a persona, a stylistic direction, the prevailing environment posed difficult questions of artistic purpose. As Kainen has pointed out, "Few young American artists knew much in the 1930s. We were poor, footloose, had never been anywhere, and had no prospects of going. The Depression had driven us to think of social change; in such an atmosphere a more than passing concern with aesthetics was tantamount to frivolity." [3] A chance acquaintanceship with Arshile Gorky during this decisive period opened the door for Kainen to new and important experiences. Gorky and Kainen would often walk together through the streets of New York while Gorky pointed out with excitement and pleasure the city's textures and colors, created by chance or weathering. On other occasions, the two, with John Graham, would go to galleries where Graham and Gorky would analyze in depth the composition and coloration of paintings while Kainen listened and observed. These talks and gallery visits were, as Kainen has said, a revelation and a formative influence. The emphasis placed by Gorky and Graham on "shapemaking and painterly authority, and on the plunge into 'enigma,' " was to leave its mark. [4]

During his rambles through the New York galleries, Kainen had seen many prints, at Keppels and other print shops. These were mainly nineteenth-century prints or, if contemporary, rather conservative etchings. Picasso, the German Expressionists, or even the more mildly advanced of the American printmakers were not widely shown. Even so, Kainen found himself increasingly drawn to the particular aesthetic qualities of prints, attracted by what he considered were their uniquely beautiful properties. Early in his studies, at age eighteen, he had tried his hand at some drypoints on aluminum plates, which he printed with a clothes wringer, but it was not until the establishment of the Federal Art Project in the mid-thirties that Kainen had any real opportunity for extensive work. Although his primary occupation at this point was with painting, Kainen was counseled by Stuart Davis to avoid the easel and mural sections of the program and instead to join the graphic arts program. "Keep your paintings," Davis said, suggesting that Kainen's work with multiple images would not only satisfy the requirements of employment but would allow him to protect unique works from being scattered or carelessly handled. Davis's advice, together with Kainen's own interest in printmaking techniques, persuaded him to try employment with the New York Graphic Arts Project, which he joined in August 1935, at the very beginning of the program.

Although the project would not be fully equipped with both etching and lithograph presses, paper, plates, and lithograph stones, and staffed by experienced printers, until early in 1936, Kainen had already created two works in 1935. These were done in lithography, a medium for which he showed an immediate affinity. His first, *Drought,* was fairly orthodox in its straightforward, controlled drawing, but in his next lithograph, *Tenement Fire* (cat. no. 1), Kainen's approach visibly loosened as he heightened the drama of the scene with expressive, broadly brushed blacks with white accents scratched in with a needle or knife. The excitement of the scene has been visually heightened by dramatic diagonals and by a realization of the possibilities in lithography for direct and vigorous handling.

From this early point on, Kainen continued to explore lithography as a painter might, working freely, expressively, and seeking new means of introducing textures and tonal nuances. Except for some technical tricks of the craft that might be picked up from those more experienced around him, Kainen developed his lithographic style by trial and error during the next few years. Apparently he was able, from the very beginning, to confront a blank stone without the fear or hesitancy that inhibits some novices, as he sought for fresh and meaningful approaches in each work. One of the most striking of many exceptionally fine prints done on the project is the very moving *Aftermath* (cat. no. 5), a strong statement in bold contrasts and expressive forms. Spiked branches of stripped trees and jutting timbers of shattered houses and fences have been drawn in intensely black, angular brushstrokes to underscore the sense of total devastation. The small figures, almost obscured by the wreckage, are empathic reminders of overwhelming human misfortune. In contrast, *River Piece* (cat. no. 12) is a quiet study in subtle grays, in which an infinite variety of tones has been built on and unified by an all-over spattering. Here the mood is poetic, formed by mist-shrouded docks, a solitary figure, the rythmic rise and fall of silhouetted pylons, and the distant skyline. In other works, such as *Loading Up* (cat. no. 10), he was more obviously fascinated with richly textured darks and lights. Working with a combination of tusche and crayon, as he often did, Kainen has scumbled and scratched the stone until we can almost feel the urban grit. Conventional perspective has been abandoned in favor of a tilted background against which simplified figures and shapes are arranged in a delightfully complex play on triangulated forms.

In his prints of the later thirties, as in his paintings, Kainen worked in simplified, rather flattened forms with a marked emphasis on shapemaking and emphatically articulated contours. The more pronounced expressive and abstract modes that would appear later in his work were now, at least in the prints, often governed by a recognition of a somewhat more natural solidity of forms, although an authoritative, calligraphic gesture is already a major element. This spontaneous gesture, as personal as a signature, and a marked preference for angular patterns, remain basic to Kainen's work, whether representational or nonobjective.

Much of Kainen's subject matter was taken from observations of the city and its life, not as actually seen, but changed and simplified. A natural empathy and compassion for humanity is evident in his scenes of workers, peddlers, and the drab inhabitants of the cafeterias and rooming houses, although he could, on occasion, turn a satirical eye on human frailties, as he did in the lithograph *Lunch* (cat. no. 3). His sympathy is most explicitly stated in scenes of real devastation, such as *Aftermath* and *Spanish Landscape with Figures* (cat. no. 9), but even these are not to be confused with the more mundane social commentaries of the thirties. True, a concern for the human condition is part of the man and the artist, and like many of his contemporaries Kainen very naturally reacted to the social and economic environment, but his works of the thirties reflect as well a growing sophistication and individuality quite unlike that of many of his contemporaries on the Federal Art Project.

The opportunity to experiment in a number of rarely used or new graphic techniques was one of the project's more positive contributions. As a painter, Kainen was attracted by the unknown possibilities of color lithography, which, until the project, was not commonly practiced in the earlier decades of this century in the United States. Russell Limbach had been making color lithographs in Ohio as early as 1927, and his presence on the project led to the establishment of a formalized section for color lithography within the program. Even before this, however, in 1937, Kainen had made his first color lithograph, *Cafeteria* (cat. no. 6), with Limbach's assistance, and continued to make four more over the next few years. Working at times in as many as five colors, Kainen used these in overlays to create a complex palette, so that these prints often appear to have been made with

Figure 2. *Cafeteria,* 1937, color lithograph, cat. no. 6.

Figure 3. Sketch for *Cafeteria,* 1936, pencil.

11

even more colors. These lovely prints, with their beautifully modulated color harmonies and deceptive simplicity of means are among his most successful prints made while he worked on the project. Kainen also worked in drypoint, etching, and woodcut, and tried his hand at the new silkscreen techniques, borrowed from the commercial printers for adaptation to the production of artists' color prints. Kainen's solo serigraph for the project, *Snowfall* (cat. no. 11), was essentially a printed painting involving thirty-two separate colors. It was time-consuming for Kainen to print the serigraph, and because other artists were waiting to use the screens, only four impressions were ever made.

By 1942 the projects were faltering and changing. At best, employment on the New York Graphic Arts Project had been precarious. Artists were fired periodically, ostensibly to free them to look for jobs, but little employment was available. To continue on the project, artists had to watch the Home Relief assignment boards, as Kainen did, until an opening in the graphic arts appeared, and then rush—by streetcar—to be the first in line.[5] Between 1935 and 1942 Kainen was fired and rehired three times. Finally, in 1942 he decided to accept the offer of a job with the Division of Graphic Arts in the Smithsonian Institution, but it was with great reluctance that he left New York and all that it represented for a young artist.

As an aide in the sparsely staffed Division of Graphic Arts, Kainen's duties were varied and included giving printing demonstrations on the department's presses. Since the improvement of his technical knowledge was an integral part of his job, he was given the go-ahead to print on his own after office hours and on Saturdays. By 1945 he was again making prints—mainly small etchings and drypoints that he could work on in odd moments and print for himself. Although the hours given to printmaking have meant less time for painting, the graphic arts have continued to hold great importance for Kainen. He is one of the few painters who maintained a constant production of prints before the renewal of interest in printmaking by painters during the past twenty years. Between 1945 and the mid-sixties Kainen produced more than fifty prints while taking on increasingly substantial responsibilities in the Division of Graphic Arts, in addition to painting, teaching, writing, and lecturing. Although Kainen continued to show his paintings in one-man and group shows in New York and Washington during these years, his prints of this period are scarcely known outside Washington. Kainen had made a difficult decision when he was promoted to curator of the Division of Graphic Arts in 1946. In his new position as head of a department, he was brought into much closer association with print dealers and other curators around the country. Even the slightest suggestion of presumption on professional contacts was unthinkable for a man of Kainen's sensibilities. Consequently he dropped out, in a sense, from the national print scene. He exhibited locally and occasionally submitted prints to national competitions, but only when he was not personally acquainted with the jurors—a situation that became increasingly less frequent. Ironically, as his reputation grew as a leading scholar and authority on the prints of others, his position as a printmaker became, by deliberate withdrawal, more obscure.

Kainen continued to draw on his observations and experiences of city life for many of his prints of the forties and early fifties, although he now added portraits, figure studies, landscapes, and an occasional nonobjective work. As in the paintings of a few years earlier, the architecture of the city, particularly the older buildings of slum streets and the once-elegant Victorian residences attracted him. The elaborate, often fantastic decorations of Victorian facades, cupolas, and turrets were visually fascinating. At the same time they suggested the romantic, at times the almost pathetically overreaching aspirations of another age, when their makers sought to

Figure 4. *The Tower,* 1947, etching, cat. no. 16.

Figure 5.   Sketch, 1946, pencil.

give importance and a sense of traditional substance to their creations by piling on borrowed decorations from other times and places. These fanciful contours and silhouettes were the springboard for many prints in which the full calligraphic spontaneity of Kainen's line is given free play. Kainen's sketches of the buildings only served as visual reminders. Beginning with only the slightest notation of form, he made decisions and allowed the composition to grow while working directly on the plate. The use of a diamond point, which easily cuts through copper, allowed an even greater ease of drawing in his drypoints of these years. In works such as *Peddler* (cat. no. 20), space and structure become secondary to the fragmented shapes and wonderfully inventive lines of his kaleidoscopic view of street elements. In the etched *Street at Night* (cat. no. 27), line is more controlled, yet still animated in its barely descriptive meanderings that begin in the buildings and are then repeated with echoing variations in the street forms. Again, line, vigorous yet restrained, is used to describe with a precise and graceful simplicity such figure studies as *Bertha Resting* or *Betty*, or becomes more complex in the elegant forms of the enigmatic *Pilgrim* (cat. no. 15) and *Vesta* (cat. no. 17).

Even when Kainen had moved toward a more nonobjective preoccupation with expressive form and color in his paintings of the late forties and fifties, his prints retained their linear qualities and remained within a more natural world of the architecture, people, streets, and parks of the city. Only in the complex overlays of luminous tones and forms of his abstract aquatints do we find the same broadened, energetic, and twisting lines of his paintings.

In many respects, the impulses that shape Kainen's paintings and prints of the late fifties and sixties coalesce most exactly in his woodcuts of the early sixties. The broad, planar quality of the woodcut lent itself admirably to the monumental figures that appeared in Kainen's paintings at that time. Earlier, in the late fifties, there had been a suggestion in his paintings of a return to the figure, but there was now a new emphasis on massive, broadly conceived forms. In the woodcuts, these solitary, pensive, and often rather mysterious figures have been vigorously cut with an expressive force that produces sharply angled or boldly curved contours and complex inner structures. They have at once a strong sense of solidity of form as well as flattened patterns that are so often a part of Kainen's work.

Kainen had often wanted to resume his work in lithography, particularly color lithography, but until the sixties there was little opportunity. With his retirement from the Smithsonian Institution in 1970, and his decision to stop teaching, Kainen now had enough free time to return to this idea. He had met Jack Lemon, founder of the Landfall Press in Chicago, and in 1972 decided to go there for several days. The working milieu proved to be congenial and Kainen produced several lithographs in both black and white and color that year. The year represents a decisive turning point in Kainen's printmaking as successive visits to the workshop have yielded a remarkable outpouring of sumptuously colored lithographs.

The lithographs are closely related to the new direction Kainen's painting took in the late sixties—a nonobjective exploration of formal relationships between large, geometric shapes and flat, unbroken areas of shimmering, vibrant color. Similar qualities in color are not easily achievable in lithography; so much depends on subtle overlays, the precise mixing of colors, or minute adjustments that allow suggestions or the edge of a color to show through. The fact that lithographic washes are not always easily held during printing increases the difficulties. These lithographs succeed because the artist has approached them directly, making full use of the free, painterly stroke permitted by tusche washes. A sense of confident exhilaration pervades the prints as the artist seems to revel in color and unrestrained gesture.

13

Figure 6. Jacob Kainen working in studio at home, 1976.

Although we know that these are the result of preliminary sketches in oil washes and predetermined decisions, Kainen has sustained the original freshness and verve and avoided a too conspicuous or controlled perfection.

At times in these lithographs the color seems to flow over the paper in large areas, as in *Hesperus* (cat. no. 52), and creates ambiguous spaces through which cryptic symbols and forms move or hang suspended. In others, like *Alma* and *Kingmaker* (cat. nos. 40 and 48), color is used as pure form to construct emblematic shapes composed of the same enigmatic symbols and geometric figures, the surfaces enlivened with seemingly accidental blots or the unexpected introduction of a small area of color or pattern that jogs the senses. Although more carefully planned than many of Kainen's etchings, these lithographs are as much a product of an intellectual and emotional openness, without a strictly preconceived imagery, as are the original oil sketches. Kainen welcomes the accidental or spontaneous, and changes and new decisions are made during the course of creation. This same openness allows emotional overtones to grow with the work as more formal aspects of the print or painting progress. Kainen has said that his approach is oblique, "while creating the work, I think of forms and colors and let the subject as such dictate itself without illustrative connotations."[6] Each work thus becomes a kind of personal odyssey, a search for both self and creative statement.

For much the same reasons, Kainen likes the uncertainties of intaglio techniques and the direct involvement they demand. As the etching or aquatint grows and changes, or "suffers," as Kainen puts it, under the artist's hand, it takes on a life of its own. Kainen delights in this "spontaneity and the after thoughts" and in the resulting accumulation of layers and densities of ink, line, and tone that offer a sensual richness of surface. In the recent series of intaglios done in his new workshop at home, Kainen has preferred to work mainly in black and white. On a few occasions, however, he has added a subtle and warm second color and has considered trying some work in color intaglio in the near future.

As this catalog goes to press, Jacob Kainen is working at the print shops of Desjobert and Lacourière et Frélaut in Paris. At the latter shop, working with Jacques Frélaut, he is moving finally into a fuller use of color intaglio. Kainen long ago mastered the technical requirements of printmaking; the process of creation for him, his open and willing commitment to the experiential, are ever new.

Notes

1. Frank Getlein, "Jacob Kainen Show at Corcoran Gallery," *Washington Sunday Star,* March 3, 1963.
2. Quoted in Florence S. Berryman, "Art and Artists," *Washington Sunday Star,* May 29, 1949, p. C-2.
3. Jacob Kainen, "Memories of Arshile Gorky," *Arts* (May 1976): 97.
4. Ibid., 98.
5. For a full description of the New York Graphic Arts Project, see Jacob Kainen, "The Graphic Arts Division of the WPA Federal Art Project," in *The New Deal Art Projects: An Anthology of Memoirs,* ed. Francis V. O'Connor (Washington, D.C.: Smithsonian Institution Press, 1972), pp. 155-75.
6. Quoted in *Art in Washington, 1969 Calendar & Diary,* ed. Leslie Judd Ahlander (Washington, D.C.: Acropolis Books, 1968).

Catalog of the Exhibition

The catalog is arranged chronologically and entries are listed alphabetically by title within each year.

Dimensions are in inches, height preceding width, and are of the plate for intaglio prints and of the image for lithographs and serigraphs, unless otherwise indicated. All works are on paper.

Through the generosity of the artist and of Mrs. B. S. Cole, we have been able to draw on the holdings of the National Collection of Fine Arts for many of the prints in the exhibition. We are most grateful to the Baltimore Museum of Art and to the artist for lending additional works.

A checklist of all of Jacob Kainen's known prints follows the catalog of the exhibition. The number that follows the title of each print in the catalog refers to the checklist (CL) number.

1. **Tenement Fire** (CL no. 2)   1935
lithograph
12¼ x 9¼
Lent by the artist

2. **Dock Scene** (CL no. 4)   1936
lithograph
7¾ x 10⅝
Lent by The Baltimore Museum of Art;
Gift of WPA Art Program

3. **Lunch** (CL no. 5)   1936
lithograph
12⅝ x 10³⁄₁₆
Lent by the artist

4. **Money Ball** (CL no. 6)   1936
lithograph
9¹³⁄₁₆ x 13¹⁵⁄₁₆
National Collection of Fine Arts; Gift of
the artist

5. **Aftermath** (CL no. 10)   1937
hand-colored lithograph
13 x 17¾ (uneven image)
Lent by the artist

6. **Cafeteria** (CL no. 11)   1937
color lithograph
12 x 16¼
National Collection of Fine Arts; Gift of
the artist

7. **Banana Man** (CL no. 22)   1938
color lithograph
10¹⁵⁄₁₆ x 13⅜
National Collection of Fine Arts; Gift of
the artist

8. **Cement Mixer** (CL no. 24)   1938
color lithograph
12 x 16
National Collection of Fine Arts; Gift of
the artist

9. **Spanish Landscape with Figures**
(CL no. 29)   1938
lithograph
14⅜ x 10⅞
National Collection of Fine Arts; Gift of
the artist

10. **Loading Up** (CL no. 33)   1939
lithograph
14½ x 11
National Collection of Fine Arts; Gift of
the artist

11. **Snowfall** (CL no. 35)   1939
serigraph
11⅞ x 16¹⁄₁₆
Lent by the artist

12. **River Piece** (CL no. 40)   1940
lithograph
10 x 14
National Collection of Fine Arts; Gift of
the artist

13. **The Midnight Ride**
(CL no. 45)   1945
etching and aquatint
6 x 7¼
Lent by the artist

14. **Self Portrait with Drypoint Needle**
(CL no. 46)   1945
drypoint
9¾ x 7⅞
Lent by the artist

15. **Pilgrim** (CL no. 54)   1947
etching
5⅞ x 4⅞
Lent by the artist

16. **The Tower** (CL no. 57)   1947
etching
3¹¹⁄₁₆ x 2¾
Lent by the artist

17. **Vesta** (CL no. 58)   1947
etching and aquatint
10 x 7⅜
Lent by the artist

18. **The Avenue** (CL no. 59)   1948
etching
7⅞ x 6³⁄₁₆
Lent by the artist

19. **The Island** (CL no. 60)   1948
drypoint and aquatint
8¹³⁄₁₆ x 11⅞
Lent by the artist

20. Peddler (CL no. 62)   1948
etching and drypoint
7^{15}⁄$_{16}$ x 9^{13}⁄$_{16}$
Lent by the artist

21. Street with Dog Walker
(CL no. 64)   1948
etching
3 x 4
Lent by the artist

22. Marine Apparition
(CL no. 68)   1949
aquatint
8⅞ x 11⅞
Lent by the artist

23. Pilgrim (CL no. 72)   1949
woodcut
15 x 12^{1}⁄$_{16}$
Lent by the artist

24. Residential Turrets
(CL no. 74)   1949
drypoint
7^{13}⁄$_{16}$ x 9⅞
Lent by the artist

25. Store Front (CL no. 75)   1949
drypoint
6 x 7^{15}⁄$_{16}$
Lent by the artist

26. Shores of Darkness
(CL no. 78)   1950
soft ground etching, aquatint, and
roulette
8⅞ x 11⅞
Lent by the artist

27. Street at Night (CL no. 79)   1950
etching
7^{1}⁄$_{16}$ x 5⅛
Lent by the artist

28. Street with Bicycle
(CL no. 80)   1951
drypoint
3^{15}⁄$_{16}$ x 3
Lent by the artist

29. The Corner Store
(CL no. 89)   1955
drypoint
7⅞ x 9⅞
Lent by the artist

30. Intersection (CL no. 90)   1955
woodcut
12⅛ x 15⅛
Lent by the artist

31. Pedestrians (CL no. 91)   1955
drypoint
7⅞ x 6
Lent by the artist

32. Head (CL no. 93)   1960
woodcut
15⅛ x 12^{1}⁄$_{16}$
Lent by the artist

33. The Midnight Sun
(CL no. 92)   1960
etching, drypoint, and engraving
11^{13}⁄$_{16}$ x 14¾
Lent by the artist

34. Boy Telephoning (CL no. 94)   1964
woodcut
15¾ x 15½
Lent by the artist

35. Girl with Ear Pendants
(CL no. 95)   1965
woodcut
16^{9}⁄$_{16}$ x 11⅜
Lent by the artist

36. Night Walk (CL no. 97)   1965
woodcut
22 x 15½
Lent by the artist

37. The Court (CL no. 98)   1966
woodcut
13^{1}⁄$_{16}$ x 12⅛
Lent by the artist

38. Mona (CL no. 100)   1968
woodcut
21⅛ x 17⅝
Lent by the artist

39. Mr. Kafka (CL no. 103)   1970
etching, aquatint, and engraving
19⅝ x 15⅞
National Collection of Fine Arts

40. Alma (CL no. 104)   1972
color lithograph
25¼ x 19¹⁄₁₆
National Collection of Fine Arts; Gift of
Mrs. B. S. Cole

41. Fabrizio (CL no. 107)   1972
serigraph
25½ x 17⅞
National Collection of Fine Arts; Gift of
Mrs. B. S. Cole

42. Color Guard (CL no. 113)   1973
color lithograph
28⅛ x 20 (uneven image)
National Collection of Fine Arts; Gift of
the artist

43. Dusk—Leningrad
(CL no. 120)   1973
color lithograph
28 x 20
National Collection of Fine Arts; Gift of
Mrs. B. S. Cole

44. The Fabulous Manipulator
(CL no. 114)   1973
color lithograph
21¼ x 26⅛
National Collection of Fine Arts; Gift of
Mrs. B. S. Cole

45. Hot Spots (CL no. 115)   1973
color lithograph
28¼ x 20 (uneven image)
National Collection of Fine Arts; Gift of
the artist

46. Hot Spots
oil wash and chalk
25⅛ x 19 (sheet)
Lent by the artist

47. Invader (CL no. 117)   1973
lithograph
28¾ x 20⅜ (uneven image)
National Collection of Fine Arts; Gift of
Mrs. B. S. Cole

48. Kingmaker (CL no. 118)   1973
color lithograph
25¼ x 19¼
Lent by the artist

49. Standard Bearer
(CL no. 126)   1973
color lithograph
28⅜ x 20⁷⁄₁₆
National Collection of Fine Arts; Gift of
the artist

50. Advance Man (CL no. 127)   1974
color lithograph
25¼ x 19½
National Collection of Fine Arts; Gift of
the artist

51. Flagman (CL no. 128)   1974
color lithograph
25¼ x 19¼
National Collection of Fine Arts; Gift of
the artist

52. Hesperus (CL no. 130)   1974
color lithograph
22⅛ x 28¼
National Collection of Fine Arts; Gift of
the artist

53. Power Play (CL no. 131)   1974
color lithograph
20¼ x 28¹⁄₁₆
National Collection of Fine Arts; Gift of
the artist

54. Secretary General
(CL no. 132)   1974
color lithograph
28 x 20 (uneven image)
Lent by the artist

55. Agent Provocateur
(CL no. 134)   1975
lithograph
18¾ x 26
Lent by the artist

56. Cloudy Trophy (CL no. 135)   1975
color etching, aquatint, and drypoint
19⅞ x 15¾
Lent by the artist

57. Cloudy Trophy 1975
pen and ink, oil wash, and tempera
20 x 16 (sheet)
Lent by the artist

58. The Last Fling (CL no. 136) 1975
color lithograph
30 x 20 (uneven image)
Lent by the artist

59. Overseer (CL no. 137) 1975
drypoint and roulette
7⅞ x 5⅞
Lent by the artist

60. Plunger (CL no. 138) 1975
drypoint and roulette
8¾ x 11⅝
Lent by the artist

61. Coeur de Vey I (CL no. 140) 1976
color lithograph
22½ x 16¼
Lent by the artist

62. Coeur de Vey II (CL no. 141) 1976
color lithograph
19¼ x 15¼
Lent by the artist

63. Letter From Tblisi
(CL no. 145) 1976
etching and soft ground etching
7¾ x 5¹⁵⁄₁₆
Lent by the artist

64. Masquerade (CL no. 146) 1976
color etching and aquatint
19¾ x 15¹¹⁄₁₆
Lent by the artist

65. Mr. Trouble (CL no. 147) 1976
etching, engraving, and aquatint
17⅝ x 13¾
Lent by the artist

Figure 7.   *Banana Man,* 1938, color lithograph, cat. no. 7.

Checklist of Prints

I am most grateful to Jacob Kainen and to his wife, Ruth, for their generous assistance in compiling this checklist. Their willingness to search through numerous proofs, to locate missing impressions, and to lend prints for documentation and photography has been cheerfully unfailing. Their own lists of known works have been an invaluable basis for this one.

Every attempt has been made to locate an impression of all the known prints by Jacob Kainen. Unfortunately, impressions of a few of the works done while Kainen was with the Graphic Arts Project of the Works Progress Administration (WPA) have been scattered and lost. Surviving impressions may exist, and we would appreciate information on any prints not reproduced or listed in the checklist.

Prints have been arranged chronologically and, within each year, alphabetically by title. An index of titles follows the checklist.

Prints produced while Kainen worked on the Federal Art Project were dated in some instances at a much later time and to the best recollection of the artist. Edition sizes for these works are only approximate because no records exist. Lithographs were usually printed in editions of twenty-five, plus three proofs for the artist, before the stone was resurfaced, but larger or smaller editions were not unknown. For other prints, only the size of the actual edition has been noted. In most cases, a few working proofs do exist for these in the collection of the artist.

Dimensions are in inches, height preceding width, and are of the plate for intaglio prints, and of the image for lithographs and serigraphs, unless otherwise indicated. All works are on paper.

Public collections (Coll) containing prints by Jacob Kainen are specified in the checklist entries; private collections are not included.

Janet A. Flint

1

1. Drought 1935
lithograph, 8⅛ x 10¹⁵⁄₁₆
Edition: approximately 25
WPA: Federal Art Project
Note: Print is artist's first lithograph.
Coll: Brooklyn Public Library, New York; Historical
Society of Pennsylvania, Philadelphia; Queens
College Art Collection, Flushing, New York;
Washington County Museum of Fine Arts,
Hagerstown, Maryland

2. Tenement Fire 1935
lithograph, 12¼ x 9¼
Edition: approximately 25
WPA: Federal Art Project
Coll: The Baltimore Museum of Art; Krannert Art
Museum, University of Illinois, Champaign; The
Metropolitan Museum of Art, New York; The New
York Public Library, New York; The Oakland
Museum, California; Philadelphia Museum of Art;
San Francisco Museum of Art; University Gallery,
University of Minnesota, Minneapolis

2

3

0. **Dead End** 1936
lithograph, 8⅛ x 11⅛
Edition: approximately 25
WPA: Federal Art Project
Coll: The Baltimore Museum of Art; Krannert Art
Metropolitan Museum of Art, New York; The
Oakland Museum, California; Racine Art
Association, Wustum Museum of Fine Arts,
Wisconsin; San Francisco Museum of Art;
University of Kansas Museum of Art, Lawrence

4. **Dock Scene** 1936
lithograph, 7¾ x 10⅝
Edition: approximately 25
WPA: Federal Art Project
Coll: The Baltimore Museum of Art; Georgia
Museum of Art, University of Georgia, Athens;
New York State Merchant Marine Academy; The
Oakland Museum, California; San Francisco
Museum of Art; University of Kentucky Art
Gallery, Lexington

4

5

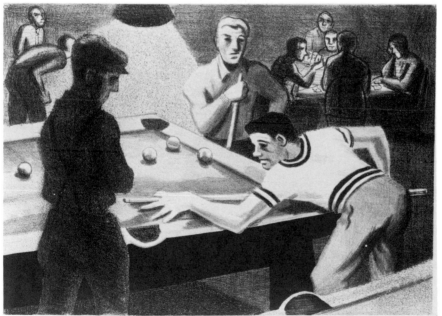

5. Lunch 1936
lithograph, 12⅝ x 10³⁄₁₆
Edition: approximately 25
WPA: Federal Art Project
Coll: The Metropolitan Museum of Art, New York;
The New York Public Library, New York

6. Money Ball 1936
lithograph, 9¹³⁄₁₆ x 13¹⁵⁄₁₆
Edition: approximately 25
WPA: Federal Art Project
Coll: National Collection of Fine Arts

6

24

7

9

7. Plasterer 1936
woodcut, 11 x 8
Edition: approximately 25
WPA: Federal Art Project
Coll: The Metropolitan Museum of Art, New York;
The New York Public Library, New York

8. Still Life 1936
color woodcut
WPA: Federal Art Project
Note: No existing impressions are known.

9. Windlass 1936
drypoint, $0^{15}/_{16}$ x $11^{7}/_{8}$
Edition: approximately 25
WPA: Federal Art Project
Coll: The New York Public Library, New York

10. Aftermath 1937
lithograph, 13 x 17¾ (uneven image)
Signed in stone, lower left:
Edition: approximately 25
WPA: Federal Art Project
Note: At least one hand-colored impression
is known.
Coll: The Baltimore Museum of Art; Brooklyn
Public Library, New York; Mulvane Art Center,
Washburn University, Topeka, Kansas; National
Collection of Fine Arts; Nebraska Art Association,
Sheldon Memorial Gallery, University of
Nebraska, Lincoln; The Oakland Museum,
California; Philadelphia Museum of Art; Racine
Art Association, Wustum Museum of Fine Arts,
Wisconsin; San Francisco Museum of Art;
University of Wyoming Art Museum, Laramie

11

12

11. Cafeteria 1937
color lithograph, 12 x 16¼
4 colors: blue, ochre, brown, gray on stone
Edition: approximately 25
WPA: Federal Art Project
Coll: The Baltimore Museum of Art; Community
Fine Arts Center, Rock Springs, Wyoming;
National Collection of Fine Arts; The Newark
Museum, New Jersey; The Oakland Museum,
California; San Francisco Museum of Art;
University Gallery of Fine Art, Ohio State
University, Columbus

12. Coffee Pot 1937
lithograph, 10½ x 13¾
Signed in stone, lower right: K
Edition: approximately 25
WPA: Federal Art Project
Coll: The Baltimore Museum of Art; Krannert Art
Museum, University of Illinois, Champaign;
National Collection of Fine Arts; The Oakland
Museum, California; San Francisco Museum
of Art

13

13. Flood   1937
lithograph, 11¼ x 14⅞
Signed in stone, lower left: J.K.
Edition: 20   Printed by Nathaniel Spreckley
Note: Nathaniel Spreckley was an elderly
English printer of lithographs, hired by the New
York Graphic Arts Project of the WPA. He
occasionally printed for artists on his own litho-
graph press.

14. Flood   1937
lithograph, 10⅝ x 13⅞
Edition: approximately 25
WPA: Federal Art Project
Coll: The Baltimore Museum of Art; Krannert Art
Museum, University of Illinois, Champaign;
The Metropolitan Museum of Art, New York; The
New York Public Library, New York; The Oak-
land Museum, California; Philadelphia Museum of
Art; Queens College Art Collection, Flushing,
New York; San Francisco Museum of Art; Walker
Art Center, Minneapolis

14

15

16

15. Girl Waiting 1937
lithograph, 14³⁄₁₆ x 10
Edition: approximately 25
WPA: Federal Art Project
Coll: The Metropolitan Museum of Art, New
York; The New York Public Library, New York;
Yale University Art Gallery, New Haven,
Connecticut

16. The Huckster 1937
lithograph, 10 x 15 (uneven image)
Edition: approximately 25
WPA: Federal Art Project
Coll: Philadelphia Museum of Art

17. Nocturne 1937
lithograph, 13⅛ x 9⁷⁄₁₆
Edition: approximately 25
WPA: Federal Art Project

17

18

19

20

18. Outskirts 1937
lithograph, 8¹³⁄₁₆ x 11¹¹⁄₁₆
Edition: approximately 25
WPA: Federal Art Project

19. Rooming House 1937
lithograph, 10½ x 13⅜
Edition: approximately 25
WPA: Federal Art Project
Coll: The Metropolitan Museum of Art, New York;
The New York Public Library, New York

20. Street Corner 1937
lithograph, 9 x 12¼ (uneven image)
Signed in stone, lower right: J.K.
Edition: approximately 25
WPA: Federal Art Project
Coll: Brooklyn Public Library, New York;
University Gallery of Fine Art, Ohio State University, Columbus

21

21. Wrecking 1937
lithograph, 9⅞ x 13⅛
Signed in stone, lower right: J K
Edition: approximately 25
WPA: Federal Art Project
Coll: The Baltimore Museum of Art; The Oakland
Museum, California; San Francisco Museum of Art

22. Banana Man 1938
color lithograph, 10¹⁵⁄₁₆ x 13⅜
5 colors: blue, orange, pale green, yellow,
gray on stone
Edition: approximately 25
WPA: Federal Art Project
Coll: The Metropolitan Museum of Art, New
York; National Collection of Fine Arts; National
Gallery of Art, Washington, D.C.; The New
York Public Library, New York; New York Uni-
versity, Institute of Fine Arts, New York;
Portland Art Gallery, Oregon; Washington County
Museum of Fine Arts, Hagerstown, Maryland

22

23

24

23. Breakfast 1938
color lithograph, 13¾ x 10¼
5 colors: brown, terra-cotta, green, gray, blue
gray on stone
Edition: approximately 25
WPA: Federal Art Project
Coll: The Baltimore Museum of Art; Millikin
University, Decatur, Illinois; The Newark Museum
New Jersey; The Oakland Museum, California;
San Francisco Museum of Art; University Gallery,
University of Minnesota, Minneapolis

24. Cement Mixer 1938
color lithograph, 12 x 16
4 colors: red, blue gray, light brown, purple
on stone
Edition: approximately 25
WPA: Federal Art Project
Coll: The Baltimore Museum of Art; East Texas
State University, Commerce; Krannert Art
Museum, University of Illinois, Champaign;
Millikin University, Decatur, Illinois; National
Collection of Fine Arts; The Oakland Museum,
California; Queens Borough Public Library,
Jamaica, New York; Queens College Art Collec-
tion, Flushing, New York; San Francisco
Museum of Art; University of Wyoming Art
Museum, Laramie

25

26

27

25. Early Evening 1938
Alternate titles: **The Shack; Be It Ever So Humble**
lithograph, 10 x 14 (uneven image)
Signed in stone, lower left: ⅃
Edition: approximately 25
WPA: Federal Art Project
Coll: The Metropolitan Museum of Art, New York;
National Collection of Fine Arts; The New York
Public Library, New York; New York Institute of
Fine Arts, New York; Yale University Art
Gallery, New Haven, Connecticut

26. Evening Recreation ca. 1939
lithograph, 14⅜ x 10¹¹⁄₁₆
Signed in stone, lower left: ⅃
Edition: approximately 25
WPA: Federal Art Project
Coll: The Metropolitan Museum of Art, New
York; National Collection of Fine Arts; The New
York Public Library, New York

27. Night Club 1938
color lithograph, 12¾ x 16⅞
4 colors: yellow, green, red, and purple on stone
Edition: approximately 25
WPA: Federal Art Project
Coll: The Newark Museum, New Jersey

33

29

30

28. Forest Pool 1938
woodcut, 11¾ x 14
Note: No existing impressions are known.

29. Spanish Landscape with Figures 1938
Alternate title: **Landscape with Figures**
lithograph, 14⅜ x 10⅞
Signed in stone, lower right: ⅃
Edition: approximately 25
WPA: Federal Art Project
Note: The original title, **Landscape with Figures,** was changed after the artist left the Federal Art Project.
Coll: Brooklyn Public Library, New York; National Collection of Fine Arts; The New York Public Library, New York; The University of Michigan Museum of Art, Ann Arbor; University of Wyoming Art Museum, Laramie; Wisconsin Union Art Collection, University of Wisconsin Madison

30. Astoria Corner 1939
lithograph, 10⅞ x 13⅜
Signed in stone, lower right: ⅃
Edition: approximately 25
WPA: Federal Art Project
Coll: The Metropolitan Museum of Art, New York; The New York Public Library, New York

31

31. Copyist 1939
lithograph, 10 x 13¾
Signed in stone, lower right: ✗
Edition: approximately 25
WPA: Federal Art Project

32. Going Home 1939
lithograph, 10⁵⁄₁₆ x 13⅞
Signed in stone, lower left: ✗
Edition: approximately 25
WPA: Federal Art Project
Coll: National Collection of Fine Arts

32

33

33. Loading Up 1939
lithograph, 14½ x 11
Edition: approximately 25
WPA: Federal Art Project
Coll: National Collection of Fine Arts

34

35

34. Sculptor 1939
lithograph, 12¹³⁄₁₆ x 9
Signed in stone, lower left: 𝒳
Edition: 25   Printed by Nathaniel Spreckley
Note: See checklist number 13.
Coll: National Collection of Fine Arts

35. Snowfall 1939
serigraph, 11⅞ x 16¹⁄₁₆
32 colors
Edition: 4
WPA: Federal Art Project
Coll: Division of Graphic Arts, National Museum
of History and Technology, Smithsonian
Institution, Washington, D.C.

36. Sunday Afternoon 1939
lithograph printed in green, 15½ x 12
Signed in stone, lower left: 𝒳
Edition: approximately 25
WPA: Federal Art Project
Note: At least one hand-colored impression is
known.
Coll: Philadelphia Museum of Art

37

36

37

37. Barber Shop 1940
lithograph, 13⅝ x 10¹⁄₁₆
Signed in stone, lower left: 𝒦
Edition: approximately 25
WPA: Federal Art Project
Coll: The Metropolitan Museum of Art, New York; National Collection of Fine Arts; The New York Public Library, New York

38. Convalescent 1940
lithograph, 10⅛ x 14
Edition: approximately 25
WPA: Federal Art Project
Coll: The Metropolitan Museum of Art, New York; The New York Public Library, New York

38

39

40

39. Morning Catch 1940
Alternate title: **The Catch**
lithograph, 10⅜ x 13¾
Signed in stone, lower right: ⅄
Edition: approximately 25
WPA: Federal Art Project
Coll: The Metropolitan Museum of Art, New
York; The New York Public Library, New York;
New York University, Institute of Fine Arts,
New York; Yale University Art Gallery, New
Haven, Connecticut

40. River Piece 1940
lithograph, 10 x 14
Signed in stone, lower center: JK
Edition: approximately 25
WPA: Federal Art Project
Coll: National Collection of Fine Arts; National
Gallery of Art, Washington, D.C.

41. Tugboat 1940
lithograph, 11⅛ x 15⅛
WPA: Federal Art Project
Note: No existing impressions are known.

42

43

42. Waitress 1940
lithograph, 10¾ x 14½
Signed in stone, lower right: 𝒦
Edition: approximately 25
WPA: Federal Art Project
Coll: The New York Public Library, New York; New York University, Institute of Fine Arts, New York; Yale University Art Gallery, New Haven, Connecticut

43. Wood-block Printer 1940
lithograph, 12⅜ x 16
Signed in stone, lower center: 𝒦
Edition: approximately 25
WPA: Federal Art Project
Coll: Historical Society of Pennsylvania, Philadelphia; National Collection of Fine Arts; The New York Public Library, New York; New York University, Institute of Fine Arts, New York

45

46

47

44. Alone
etching
Edition: approximately 25
WPA: Federal Art Project
Note: No existing impressions are known.

45. The Midnight Ride   1945
etching and aquatint, 6 x 7¼
Edition: 25   Printed by the artist

46. Self Portrait with Drypoint Needle   1945
drypoint, 9¾ x 7⅞
Edition: unique impression

47. Alter Ego   1946
drypoint, 5½ x 7⅜
Signed in plate, lower right: JK
Edition: 20   Printed by the artist

48

48. Betty 1946
etching, 7⅞ x 5⅞
Signed in plate, lower center: ✗
Edition: 30   Printed by the artist

49. Dunes and Sea 1946
etching and engraving, 2¾ x 3¾
Edition: 40   Printed by the artist
Note: Print was created as a New Year's greeting

49

50

51

50. Figurescape 1946
etching, 6⅞ x 4⁷⁄₁₆
Signed in plate, lower right: JK
Edition: 40   Printed by the artist

51. Virginia Hills 1946
drypoint, 7⁷⁄₁₆ x 10¹³⁄₁₆
Signed in plate, lower left: JK
Edition: 15   Printed by the artist
Note: The plate was executed in December 1946;
some impressions were printed in 1947 and
dated that year.
Coll: National Gallery of Art, Washington, D.C.

52. Headland 1947
etching, aquatint, and roulette, 7⅜ x 9¾
Signed in plate, lower left: 𝒳
Edition: 20   Printed by the artist
Coll: The Baltimore Museum of Art

52

53

54

53. Lakeside 1947
drypoint, 7½ x 11
Edition: approximately 8   Printed by the artist

54. Pilgrim 1947
etching, 5⅞ x 4⅞
Signed in plate, lower left: 𝒳
Edition: 50   Printed by the artist
Coll: Corcoran Gallery of Art, Washington, D.C.;
National Gallery of Art, Washington, D.C.

55

55. Self Portrait 1947
etching, 7¹³⁄₁₆ x 5⅞
Signed in plate, lower left:
Edition: 20   Printed by the artist

56. The Street 1947
etching and engraving, 5 x 5⅞
Signed in plate, lower right: 𝒦
Edition: 30   Printed by the artist

56

57

58

59

57. The Tower 1947
etching, 3¹¹⁄₁₆ x 2¾
Edition: 35   Printed by the artist
Note: Print was created as a New Year's greetir

58. Vesta 1947
etching and aquatint, 10 x 7⅜
Signed in plate, lower left: 𝕶
Edition: 35   Printed by the artist
Coll: Carnegie Institute, Pittsburgh; National
Gallery of Art, Washington, D.C.

59. The Avenue 1948
etching, 7⅞ x 6³⁄₁₆
Signed in plate, lower left: 𝕶
Edition: 25   Printed by the artist
Coll: National Gallery of Art, Washington, D.C.

60

60. The Island   1948
drypoint and aquatint, 8¹³⁄₁₆ x 11⅞
Signed in plate, lower right: ⅃
Edition: 30   Printed by the artist

61. The Island #2   1948
drypoint and aquatint, 8⅞ x 12⅞
Edition: 20   Printed by the artist

61

62. Peddler 1948
etching and drypoint, $7^{15}/_{16}$ x $9^{13}/_{16}$
Signed in plate, lower left: 𝒦
Edition: 30   Printed by the artist

63

64

63. Self Portrait with Pipe 1948
drypoint, 5³⁄₁₆ x 4½
Signed in plate, lower left: ℋ /48
Edition: 15 Printed by the artist

64. Street with Dog Walker 1948
etching, 3 x 4
Edition: 40 Printed by the artist

65. The Walk 1948
etching, 4 x 3
Signed in plate, lower left: ℋ
Edition: 25 Printed by the artist
Note: Print was created as a New Year's greeting.

65

49

66

67

66. Downtown Spire 1949
Alternate title: **Downtown Square**
drypoint, 10 x 6¹⁵⁄₁₆
Signed in plate, lower left: JK
Edition: 25   Printed by the artist

67. Jozef Pielage 1949
drypoint, 7⅞ x 9¾
Signed in plate, lower left: JK/1949
Edition: approximately 5   Printed by the artist

68

68. Marine Apparition 1949
aquatint, 8⅞ x 11⅞
Edition: 30   Printed by the artist
Coll: Library of Congress, Washington, D.C.;
National Gallery of Art, Washington, D.C.

69. The Night Obscure 1949
drypoint and aquatint, 11⅞ x 8⅞
Signed in plate, lower right: ⅃𝒦
Edition: approximately 10   Printed by the
artist

69

51

70

71

70. The Park   1949
Alternate title: **Lakeside Park**
drypoint, 6 x 7⅞
Signed in plate, lower left: $\mathcal{K}$
Edition: 25   Printed by the artist

71. Park Phenomena   1949
drypoint, 7¹⁵⁄₁₆ x 9⅞
Signed in plate, lower left: $\mathcal{K}$
Edition: 20   Printed by the artist

72. Pilgrim 1949
woodcut, 15 x 12¹⁄₁₆
Signed in block, lower left: 𝒦
Edition: 60   Printed by the artist
Note: An edition of twenty was originally planned
and a few were numbered accordingly.

73

74

73. Residential Facade   1949
drypoint, 7⅞ x 5¹⁵⁄₁₆
Signed in plate, lower left: ⅄
Edition: 20   Printed by the artist
Coll: National Gallery of Art, Washington, D.C.

74. Residential Turrets   1949
drypoint, 7¹³⁄₁₆ x 9⅞
Signed in plate, lower left: ⅄
Edition: 30   Printed by the artist
Coll: National Gallery of Art, Washington, D.C.

75

75. Store Front   1949
drypoint, 6 x 7¹⁵⁄₁₆
Signed in plate, lower left: 𝒦
Edition: 20   Printed by the artist

76. Street Breakers   1949
drypoint, 7⅛ x 10⅞
Signed in plate, lower left: 𝒦
Edition: 27   Printed by the artist

76

77

77. Tree and Iron Gate 1949
drypoint, 7⅞ x 5⅞
Signed in plate, lower left: 𝒦
Edition: 30   Printed by the artist

78. Shores of Darkness 1950
soft ground etching, aquatint, and roulette,
8⅞ x 11⅞
Edition: 30   Printed by the artist
Coll: Library of Congress, Washington, D.C.

78

79

79. Street at Night   1950
etching, 7$\frac{1}{16}$ x 5$\frac{1}{8}$
Edition: 35   Printed by the artist

80. Street with Bicycle   1951
drypoint, 3$\frac{15}{16}$ x 3
Signed in plate, lower right: 𝒦
Edition: 35   Printed by the artist
Note: Print was created as a New Year's greeting.

80

81

82

83

81. Sun in the Hills 1951
woodcut and color stencil, 12¼ x 15⅛ (uneven image)
Edition: unique impression   Printed by the artist

82. Sun in the Hills 1951
aquatint, 8⅞ x 11¹³⁄₁₆
Edition: 20   Printed by the artist

83. Bertha Resting 1952
drypoint, 5¹³⁄₁₆ x 9⅜
Signed in plate, lower right:
Edition: 30   Printed by the artist

84

84. Reading in Bed 1952
etching, 7⅞ x 9¾
Signed in plate, lower left: ✗
Edition: 40   Printed by the artist
Coll: National Gallery of Art, Washington, D.C.

85. Street with Shopper 1952
Alternate title: **Shopper**
etching, 9¹³⁄₁₆ x 7¹⁵⁄₁₆
Signed in plate, lower left: ✗
Edition: 2 impressions   Printed by the artist

85

86

86. Stranger in the Gates 1953
color woodcut, 16¾ x 21⅛
5 colors: green, black, brown, blue, red
Edition: 6   Printed by the artist
Note: Two variant impressions, printed in black and red, exist.

87. Transit 1953
etching and aquatint, 7¹⁵⁄₁₆ x 9⅞
Edition: 15   Printed by the artist
Note: A variant impression exists in which an additional color, burnt orange, has been used with black in a single printing from one plate.

87

88

88. Woman Reading   1953
Alternate title: **Reader**
drypoint, 5⅞ x 3¹⁵⁄₁₆
Signed in plate, lower left: ꓘ
Edition: 25   Printed by the artist

89. The Corner Store   1955
drypoint, 7⅞ x 9⅞
Signed in plate, lower right: ꓘ
Edition: 35   Printed by the artist

89

90

91

90. Intersection 1955 (first version)
woodcut, 12⅛ x 15⅛
Edition: 30   Printed by the artist

90a. Intersection 1955 (second version)
woodcut, 12⅛ x 15⅛
Edition: 30   Printed by the artist
Note: This print is almost identical to the first
version. It differs slightly in treatment, and the
lamp post no longer appears.

91. Pedestrians 1955
Alternate title: **The Pedestrian**
drypoint, 7⅞ x 6
Signed in plate, lower left: 𝒦
Edition: 35   Printed by the artist

92. The Midnight Sun 1960
etching, drypoint, and engraving, 11¹³⁄₁₆ x 14¾
Edition: 30   Printed by the artist

92

93. Head 1960
woodcut, 15⅛ x 12¹⁄₁₆
Edition: 4 impressions   Printed by the artist

94

94. Boy Telephoning 1964
woodcut, 15¾ x 15½
Edition: 30   Printed by the artist
Coll: Library of Congress, Washington, D.C.;
National Collection of Fine Arts

95

95. Girl with Ear Pendants   1965
woodcut, 16⁹⁄₁₆ x 11³⁄₈
Edition: 30   Printed by the artist

96. Midnight 1965
woodcut, 15⁹⁄₁₆ x 22¼
Edition: 30   Printed by the artist
Note: Two blocks have been used in printing
the edition of thirty, one block for the head and
another for the background.
Coll: National Collection of Fine Arts; National
Gallery of Art, Washington, D.C.

96

97

97. Night Walk 1965
woodcut, 22 x 15½
Edition: 30   Printed by the artist
Note: In addition to the regular edition of thirty
in black, four impressions were printed in two
colors, blue and brown, from two blocks.

98

98. The Court 1966
woodcut, 13$\frac{1}{16}$ x 12$\frac{1}{8}$
Edition: 50   Printed by the artist

99. The Golden Calf 1968
Alternate title: **Second Commandment**
lithograph, 18$\frac{1}{16}$ x 14
Edition: 150   Printed at George C. Miller
and Son, Inc., New York, by Burr Miller
Note: Artist was commissioned to produce this
edition by the Solomon Schecter Day School in
Washington, D.C.

99

67

100

101

100. Mona 1968
woodcut, 21⅛ x 17⅝
Edition: 20   Printed by the artist
Coll: Dimock Gallery, George Washington
University, Washington, D.C.

101. No Dominion 1968
lithograph, 21⅞ x 29¹⁵⁄₁₆ (sheet)
Edition: 150   Printed at Mourlot, New York
Note: Commissioned by Strike 400 of Washington
D.C., to produce an edition of 375, plus twenty-
five proofs. When the organization went out of
business, after thirty-five impressions had been
sold, the remaining 340 were returned to the
artist, who reduced the edition to 150 impressions
which were renumbered beginning with 36/150.
The remaining prints were destroyed. The twenty-
five proofs were never returned to the artist.
Coll: Library of Congress, Washington, D.C.;
National Collection of Fine Arts

102

102. Abraham 1970
serigraph, 25½ x 18½
4 colors: black, rust, orange, purple
Edition: 35   Printed at Workshop, Inc.,
Washington, D.C., by Lou Stovall and the artist
Coll: National Collection of Fine Arts

103. Mr. Kafka 1970
etching, aquatint, and engraving, 19⅝ x 15⅞
Edition: 25   Printed by the artist
Coll: National Collection of Fine Arts

103

104. Alma 1972
color lithograph, 25¼ x 19¹⁄₁₆
4 colors: red on stone; pink, blue, yellow on
three aluminum plates
Edition: 35   Printed at Landfall Press, Chicago,
by Jerry Raidiger
Coll: The Achenbach Foundation for Graphic
Arts, The Fine Arts Museums of San Francisco;
National Collection of Fine Arts

105

106

105. The Apprentice   1972
color lithograph, 25 x 19¼
3 colors: green, blue, pink on three aluminum plates
Edition: 35   Printed at Landfall Press, Chicago, by Jerry Raidiger
Coll: National Collection of Fine Arts

106. The Enforcer   1972
lithograph, 27¹⁄₁₆ x 19⅛
Edition: 35   Printed at Landfall Press, Chicago, by Jerry Raidiger and Barbara Stifft
Coll: National Collection of Fine Arts

107. Fabrizio   1972
serigraph, 25½ x 17⅞
5 colors: rose, yellow, orange, blue, lavender
Edition: 35   Printed at Workshop, Inc., Washington, D.C., by Lou Stovall
Coll: The Baltimore Museum of Art; National Collection of Fine Arts

71

107

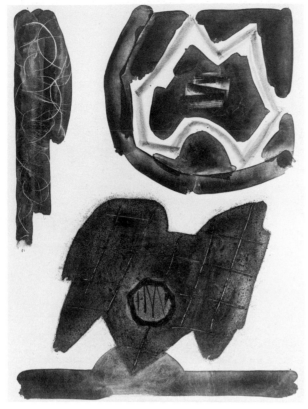

108

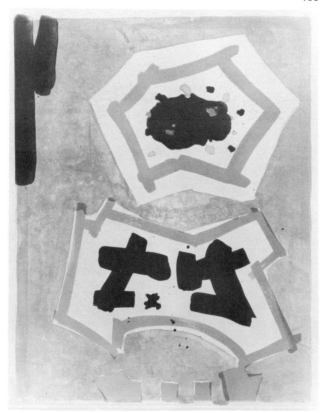

108. Flightmaster 1972
lithograph, 27¼ x 19¼ (uneven image)
Edition: 35   Printed at Landfall Press, Chicago,
by Jerry Raidiger and Barbara Stifft
Coll: National Collection of Fine Arts

109. The Great Shah 1972
color lithograph, 25⅜ x 19⅛
3 colors: yellow on stone; red, gray on two
aluminum plates
Edition: 35   Printed at Landfall Press, Chicago,
by Jerry Raidiger and David Keister
Coll: National Collection of Fine Arts

109

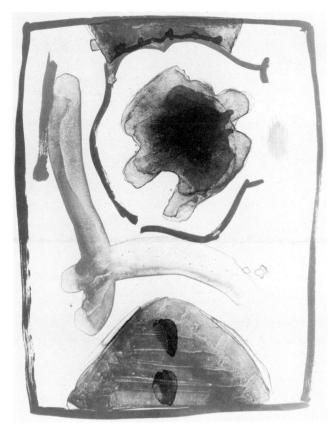

110

110. Secret Agent 1972
color lithograph, 22⅝ x 16½
3 colors: yellow on stone; red, blue on two
aluminum plates
Edition: 35   Printed at Landfall Press, Chicago,
by Jerry Raidiger
Coll: Grunwald Center for the Graphic Arts,
University of California at Los Angeles; National
Collection of Fine Arts; University of Iowa
Museum of Art, Iowa City

111. Starbuck I 1972
color lithograph, 25½ x 19¾
4 colors: blue, gray, red, yellow on four aluminum
plates
Edition: 35   Printed at Landfall Press, Chicago,
by Jerry Raidiger and Barbara Stifft
Coll: The Art Institute of Chicago; National
Collection of Fine Arts; National Gallery of Art,
Washington, D.C.

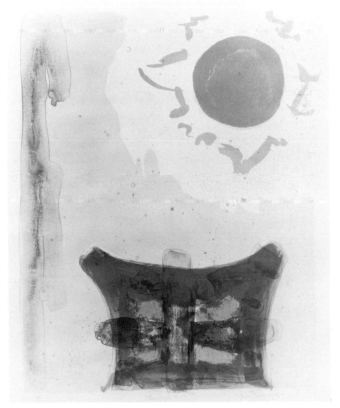

111

112

113

114

112. Anacharsis 1973
lithograph, 29 x 20¼ (uneven image)
Edition: 50   Printed at George C. Miller and Son, Inc., New York, by Burr Miller
Coll: The Achenbach Foundation for Graphic Arts, The Fine Arts Museums of San Francisco; Grunwald Center for the Graphic Arts, University of California at Los Angeles; National Collection of Fine Arts; National Gallery of Art, Washington, D.C.; University of Iowa Museum of Art, Iowa City

113. Color Guard 1973
color lithograph, 28⅛ x 20 (uneven image)
5 colors: ochre, red, blue, yellow, white on five aluminum plates
Edition: 50   Printed at Landfall Press, Chicago, by David Keister
Coll: The Brooklyn Museum, New York; National Collection of Fine Arts

114. The Fabulous Manipulator 1973
color lithograph, 21¼ x 26⅛
5 colors: light red, red, blue, yellow, gray on five aluminum plates
Edition: 50   Printed at Landfall Press, Chicago, by Jack Lemon
Coll: National Collection of Fine Arts

74

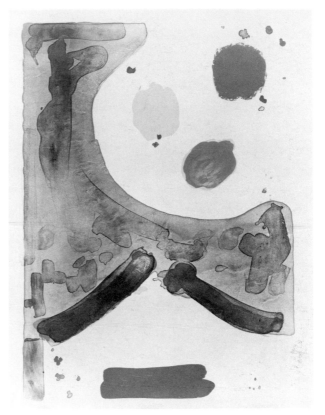

115

115. Hot Spots   1973
color lithograph, 28¼ x 20 (uneven image)
3 colors: red, blue on two stones; yellow on
aluminum plate
Edition: 50   Printed at Landfall Press, Chicago,
by Jack Lemon and David Keister
Coll: National Collection of Fine Arts

116. Hunter   1973
lithograph, 30⅛ x 22½ (sheet)
Edition: 10   Printed at the University of
Maryland, College Park, by Alan Ohambero
Coll: University of Maryland Art Gallery, College
Park

116

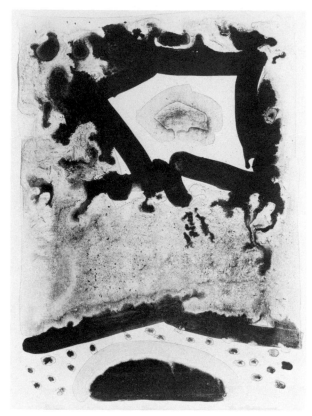

117

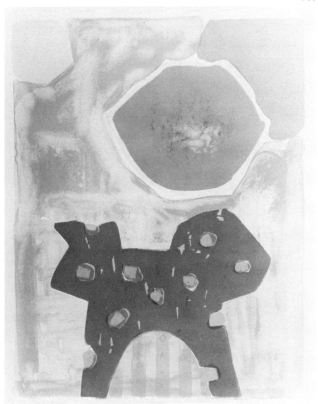

117. Invader 1973
lithograph, 28¾ x 20⅜ (uneven image)
Edition: 50   Printed at George C. Miller and
Son, Inc., New York, by Burr Miller
Coll: The Achenbach Foundation for Graphic
Arts, The Fine Arts Museums of San Francisco;
Indianapolis Museum of Art; National Collection
of Fine Arts; National Gallery of Art, Washington,
D.C.

118. Kingmaker 1973
color lithograph, 25¼ x 19¼
8 colors: two grays, blue, yellow, red, violet
gray, transparent black, white on seven aluminum
plates
Edition: 50   Printed at Landfall Press, Chicago,
by David Panosh
Coll: The Achenbach Foundation for Graphic Arts,
The Fine Arts Museums of San Francisco

118

119

119. Rampant 1973
lithograph, 30⅛ x 23 (sheet)
Edition: 50   Printed at Landfall Press, Chicago,
by Jack Lemon
Coll: The Art Institute of Chicago; The Brooklyn
Museum, New York; Indianapolis Museum of Art;
National Collection of Fine Arts; National
Gallery of Art, Washington, D.C.; University of
Iowa Museum of Art, Iowa City

Russian Suite (CL nos. 120-25)

120. Dusk—Leningrad 1973
color lithograph, 28 x 20
5 colors: gray green on stone; gray green, yellow,
red, blue on four aluminum plates
Edition: 50   Printed at Landfall Press, Chicago,
by David Keister
Coll: Museum of Modern Art, New York; National
Collection of Fine Arts

77

120

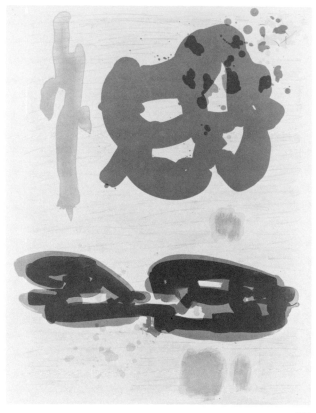

121

121. Peter the Great 1973
color lithograph, 28¾ x 21
5 colors: red, blue, yellow, gray, white on five
aluminum plates
Edition: 50   Printed at Landfall Press, Chicago,
by Jack Lemon
Coll: The Art Institute of Chicago; Grunwald
Center for the Graphic Arts, University of
California at Los Angeles; National Collection
of Fine Arts; National Gallery of Art, Washington, D.C.; University of Iowa Museum of Art,
Iowa City

122. Pushkin 1973
color lithograph, 28 x 20¾
4 colors: yellow, blue, red, transparent blue
violet on four aluminum plates
Edition: 50   Printed at Landfall Press, Chicago,
by Herb Fox
Coll: The Achenbach Foundation for Graphic
Arts, The Fine Arts Museums of San Francisco;
National Collection of Fine Arts

122

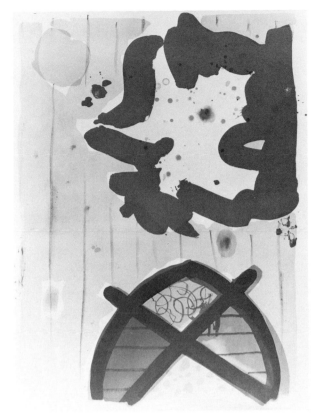

123

123. Scythian 1973
color lithograph, 29 x 20¾ (uneven image)
4 colors: red, blue, yellow, gray on four aluminum
plates
Edition: 50   Printed at Landfall Press, Chicago,
by Herb Fox
Coll: National Collection of Fine Arts

124. Tblisi Rose 1973
color lithograph, 28¼ x 20⅛
4 colors: pink on stone; red, gray, blue violet on
three aluminum plates
Edition: 50   Printed at Landfall Press, Chicago,
by Jerry Raidiger
Coll: Museum of Modern Art, New York; National
Collection of Fine Arts

124

125

125. Vladimir   1973
color lithograph, 28½ x 20¼
3 colors: red, yellow on two aluminum plates;
blue on stone
Edition: 50   Printed at Landfall Press, Chicago,
by Jack Lemon and Jerry Raidiger
Coll: National Collection of Fine Arts

126. Standard Bearer   1973
color lithograph, 28⅜ x 20⁷⁄₁₆
6 colors: gray, yellow, ochre, black on four
aluminum plates; rose, blue on two stones
Edition: 50   Printed at Landfall Press, Chicago,
by Jack Lemon and David Keister
Coll: National Collection of Fine. Arts

126

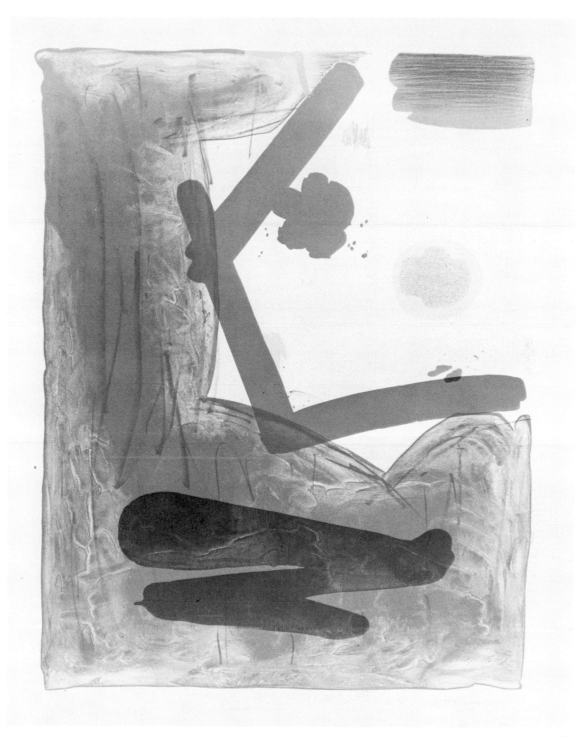

127

127. Advance Man 1974
color lithograph, 25¼ x 19½
5 colors: cold red on stone; warm red, blue,
yellow, white on four aluminum plates
Edition: 50   Printed at Landfall Press, Chicago,
by Jack Lemon and David Keister
Coll: National Collection of Fine Arts

128

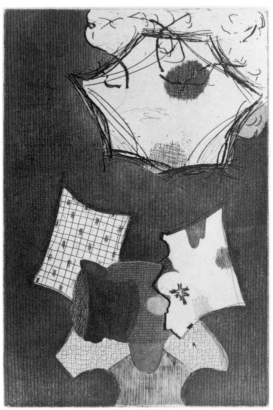

129

128. Flagman 1974
color lithograph, 25¼ x 19¼
6 colors: gray blue, dark gray on two stones;
blue green, pale terra-cotta, tan, blue on four
aluminum plates
Edition: 50   Printed at Landfall Press, Chicago
by Jack Lemon
Coll: National Collection of Fine Arts

129. Grand Master 1974
etching and aquatint, 17⅞ x 11¾
Edition: 30   Printed at Printmakers' Workshop,
Washington, D.C., by Bruce Wilson
Note: Print is one of ten prints by various
artists published as *Washington Portfolio, '74.*
Coll: The Baltimore Museum of Art; Corcoran
Gallery of Art, Washington, D.C.; Dimock
Gallery, George Washington University, Wash-
ington, D.C.; Georgetown University Collection,
Washington, D.C.; National Collection of Fine
Arts; National Gallery of Art, Washington, D.C.;
The Phillips Collection, Washington, D.C.;
University of Maryland Art Gallery, College Park;
Watkins Gallery, American University, Wash-
ington, D.C.

130

131

130. Hesperus 1974
color lithograph, 22⅛ x 28¼
7 colors: light blue on stone; violet blue, red,
gray, orange, ultramarine, white on six aluminum
plates
Edition: 50   Printed at Landfall Press, Chicago,
by Jack Lemon and Ron Wyffels
Coll: National Collection of Fine Arts; Whitney
Museum of American Art, New York

131. Power Play 1974
color lithograph, 20¼ x 28¹⁄₁₀
6 colors: gray, green, white, dark blue on four
aluminum plates; blue, red on two stones
Edition: 50   Printed at Landfall Press, Chicago,
by Jack Lemon and Ron Wyffels
Coll: National Collection of Fine Arts

132. Secretary General 1974
color lithograph, 28 x 20 (uneven image)
6 colors: red on stone; blue, gray, orange, green,
tan on five aluminum plates
Edition: 50   Printed at Landfall Press, Chicago,
by David Keister

132

133

134

133. Sheba 1974
color lithograph, 27½ x 18½ (uneven image)
5 colors: yellow, red, blue, gray, green
on five aluminum plates
Edition: 50   Printed at Landfall Press, Chicago,
by Ron Wyffels
Coll: National Collection of Fine Arts

134. Agent Provocateur 1975
lithograph, 18¾ x 26
Edition: 50   Printed at Landfall Press, Chicago,
by Jack Lemon

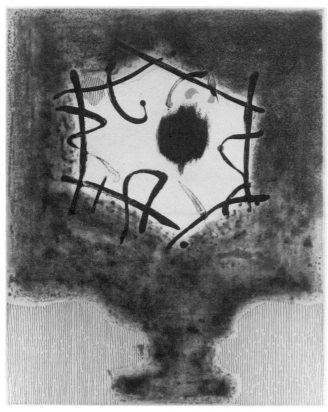

135

136

135. Cloudy Trophy 1975
color etching, aquatint, and drypoint, 19⅞ x 15¾
2 colors: black, orange on two copper plates
Edition: 40   Printed at Teaberry Press, Chicago,
by Timothy Berry

136. The Last Fling 1975
color lithograph, 30 x 20 (uneven image)
3 colors: gray on stone; terra-cotta, yellow green
on two aluminum plates
Edition: 50   Printed at Landfall Press, Chicago,
by Jack Lemon

137. Overseer 1975
drypoint and roulette, 7⅞ x 5⅞
Edition: 25   Printed by the artist

137

138. Plunger 1975
drypoint and roulette, 8¾ x 11⅝
Edition: 30   Printed by Michael Smallwood

139

139. Stranger from Omaha   1975
etching, aquatint, and soft ground etching,
9¾ x 13¹³/₁₆
Edition: 40   Printed at Teaberry Press, Chicago,
by Timothy Berry

140. Coeur de Vey I   1976
color lithograph, 22½ x 16¼
4 colors: red, rose, yellow, blue on four stones
Edition: 35   Printed at Desjobert, Paris, France

140

141

141. Coeur de Vey II 1976
color lithograph, 19¼ x 15¼
6 colors: cream, blue, gray, blue gray, pink,
pale yellow on six stones
Edition: 35   Printed at Desjobert, Paris, France

142. Coeur de Vey III 1976
color lithograph, 22½ x 16½
5 colors: two blues, yellow, tan, orange on five
stones
Edition: 35   Printed at Desjobert, Paris, France

142

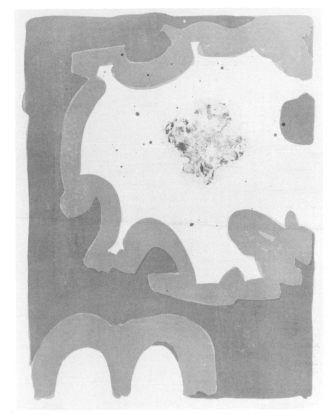

143

143. Coeur de Vey IV   1976
color lithograph, 22¼ x 16½
4 colors: pink, yellow, blue, brown on four stones
Edition: 35   Printed at Desjobert, Paris, France

144. Dr. Mabuse   1976
color etching and aquatint, 19⅞ x 16
3 colors: black, yellow, blue on three copper
plates
Edition: 30   Printed at Lacourière et Frélaut,
Paris, France

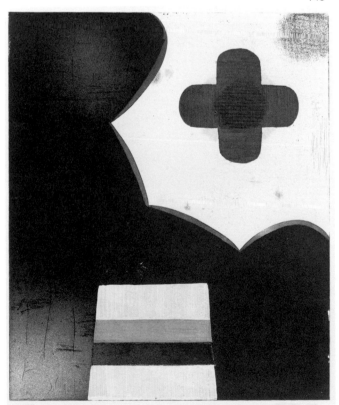

144

145

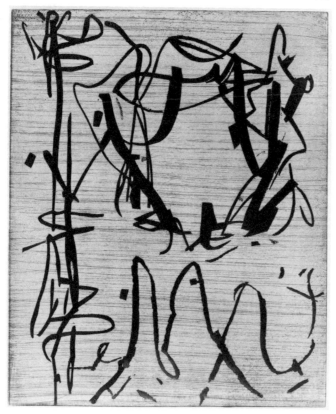

145. Letter From Tblisi   1976
etching and soft ground etching, 7¾ x 5¹⁵⁄₁₆
Edition: 40   Some impressions printed by the
artist; others by Michael Smallwood

146. Masquerade   1976
color etching and aquatint, 19¾ x 15¹¹⁄₁₆
2 colors: black, light brown on two plates
Edition: 30   Printed by Michael Smallwood
Note: The technique is adapted from a method
described to the artist by the printmaker Bernard
Greenwald.

146

147. Mr. Trouble 1976
etching, engraving, and aquatint, 17⅝ x 13¾
Edition: 40   Printed by Michael Smallwood
Note: The technique is adapted from a method
described to the artist by the printmaker Bernard
Greenwald.
Coll: National Gallery of Art, Washington, D.C.

Index by Titles of Checklist of Prints

Exhibitions

Selected one-man and group exhibitions from 1938 to 1976 are listed chronologically. Painting exhibitions have not been included.

One-Man Exhibitions

Jacob Kainen: Drawings and Lithographs, Washington, D.C.: Central Public Library, July-August 1945.
Jacob Kainen: Contemporary American Artists Series No. 7, Washington, D.C.: Corcoran Gallery of Art, May 21-September 30, 1949.
Jacob Kainen: Prints and Drawings, McLean, Virginia: Emerson Gallery, January 2-27, 1968.
Jacob Kainen: Works on Paper, Bethesda, Maryland: Hom Gallery, November 27-December 1971.

Group Exhibitions

Print Making: A New Tradition Featuring Original Color Lithography, New York: Federal Art Gallery, January 19-February 9, 1938.
99 Graphic Prints, New York: Federal Art Gallery, January 24-February 7, 1939.
1st National Lithograph Exhibition, WPA Program (Competitive), Oklahoma City, Oklahoma: Oklahoma Art Center, December 5-31, 1939.
Tho Artists Guild of Washington, Washington, D.C.: Smithsonian Institution, July 1945.
2nd Annual Print Competition, New York: Associated American Artists, August 1947.
Annual Watercolor and Print Exhibition, Oakland, California: Oakland Art Gallery, October 1947.
Annual Exhibition, Society of American Etchers, Gravers, Lithographers, and Woodcutters, New York: National Academy Galleries, the 32nd Annual, October-December 1947, and the 33rd Annual, November-December 1948.
Annual Exhibition of Works by Artists of Washington and Vicinity (later called the Annual Area Exhibition), Washington, D.C.: Corcoran Gallery of Art, 1948-1955, 1967.
National Exhibition of Prints, Washington, D.C.: Library of Congress, 1948, 1950, 1953, 1966.
Prints by Washington Artists, Washington, D.C.: The Whyte Gallery, July 6-30, 1949.
National Print Annual, Brooklyn, New York: Brooklyn Museum of Art, 1949, 1950.
New Vistas In American Art, Washington, D.C.: Howard University, 1961.

The Society of Washington Printmakers, Members' Show, Washington, D.C., and vicinity: 1966-1975.

WPA Prints: 1935-1943, Washington, D.C.: National Collection of Fine Arts, October 1-December 15, 1968.

Norwegian International Graphic Biennial: 1972, 1974.

Davidson National Print and Drawing Competition, Davidson, North Carolina: Stowe Gallery, Davidson College, 1973.

Three Contemporary Printmakers: Jacob Kainen, Albert Christ-Janer, Tadeusz Lapinski, Washington, D.C.: National Collection of Fine Arts, June 1-July 1, 1973.

International Biennial of Graphic Art, Ljubljana, Yugoslavia: 1973, 1975.

Biennial of Graphic Works and Multiples, Segovia, Spain: 1974.

International Exhibition of Graphic Art, Frechen, Germany: 1974.

Two Decades of American Prints: 1920-1940, Washington, D.C.: National Collection of Fine Arts, June 21-September 8, 1974.

Landfall Press Traveling Exhibitions: 1974-1976.

American Prints From Wood, Smithsonian Institution Traveling Exhibition Service, Washington, D.C.: 1975.

Works on Twinrocker Handmade Paper, Indianapolis, Indiana: Indianapolis Museum of Art, April 15-May 25, 1975.

WPA/FAP graphics, Smithsonian Institution Traveling Exhibition Service, Washington, D.C.: 1976.